# LOVE, LAUGHTER, AND NATURE

## A Book of Poetry

By

Mary E. Fisher

Copyright page

Spotlight PUBLISHING

# LOVE, LAUGHTER, AND NATURE

## A Book of Poetry

By

Mary E. Fisher

# TABLE OF CONTENTS

# Dedication

My undying gratitude to the smartest, kindest man I know, my husband Leonard. Without his love and support, I would never have had the courage to write this book or to have it published for the world to see.

Also, thanks go to my loving daughter Karen Montgomery, and my deceased daughter Kathy Montgomery who will never get a chance to read this.

I would also like to thank my two wonderful sisters Wilma (Willie) Taylor and Emily Watson for their encouragement.

# SUNSET

The rosy reflections of the sun
Glittering across the silken sea,
Weaving a tiny thread-like path
Of sparkling jewels for you and me.

The silhouette of the lonely pine
Standing guard upon the peaceful shore,
Like a beacon to the sailing ship…
Rest here in peace forever more.

The fragile rays of the setting sun
Spreading across the sleeping sky;
Thru the dreaming stillness of the night
Echoes the sound of a whispered sigh.

# ENDLESS LOVE

Thru the endless vast corridors
Of my mind
I continually search for but
I never find
A time my love for you
Ceases to be…

'Twas there before yesterday and
Reaches past eternity!

## FOOTPRINTS IN THE SAND

Across the sands of time
Together our footprints are seen;
'Twould be such a crime
Were the sands swept clean.

# FLYING TIME

The veil of the night is
Silently drifting away
While the world is preparing
For the coming of the day.

The morning sun slowly climbs
The stairway of the sky,
Displaying her myriad colors:
The perfect time to fly.

## ELUSIVE LOVE

Thru the velvet darkness of night
    Shines the beacon of my goal,
    Like a faint flickering light,
    Hope dwells within my soul
    That somewhere, somehow, under
    Those ever-changing Heavens above
I will find that wonderful,
Magical… elusive thing called love.

## DREAMY FEELINGS

Rainbows after a summer storm,
Dreamy nights, soft and warm.
Laughing days filled with sunshine
Your hand gently holding mine.

# DREAMS OF LOVE

We dreamed our dreams of love
While the rain was slowly falling.
We saw the rainbow fill the sky above
While the winds were softly calling

We walked, hand in hand, in the meadow
Making plans for the home we would build.
We sat in the great Oak tree's shadow
After the gentle raindrops were stilled.

We breathed the air after the showers,
The whole world felt clean and good.
We smelled the new spring flowers, and
Picked petals from the white Dogwood.

Then as the daylight began to fade and
The birds flew in the heavens above,
We talked of the plans we had made
And on that day, we found true love.

## LAST WORKING DAY

The day you have long-awaited
At last, it's finally here!
All that's left is clear your desk
And pack away your gear.
You'll fret and you'll frown
And say you'll miss us all so;
And you'll do your very best
Not to let us all know
How happy you really are
To be leaving this place.
You may even pretend to cry
And sadden your face.
You'll moan and you'll sigh
To make us all feel
That your grief and your sorrow
Both are truly real.
You think that might help us
All feel good.
We know you'd do it too
If you thought you really could.
But when you get to the part
Where you give us a big frown
We all know your great big smile
Would just let you down!

# A DAY LATE

I don't care how much you
Argue, or what you say~
I just know that this is
Still Yesterday.

## PESKY PEST

Have you ever seen
Anything like that?
That silly roach has
Just attacked my cat!

# AN OLD CHILD

Yesterday I was free and wild~
I ran and played and smiled,
My innocence had me beguiled.
Yesterday I truly was a child.

Now as the days pass quickly by
I often sit and wonder why
If time has learned to fly,
Then why, oh why, can't I?

When did my steps begin to drag?
And my body parts decide to sag?
How soon my energy begins to flag!
And even my hangnails want to snag.

This is my final edict and decree
From this day forward, it shall be
That time shall not ever be free~
To go a bit faster than me!

# DREAMING DREAMS

The country on a
Quiet summer day.
Watching the children
As they play.
Building sandcastles
On the beach.
Dreaming dreams just
Out of reach.

## DIRTY BIRDS

See that flock of birds
So high in the air?
A sign of their passing
Was left in my hair!

## DIAMONDS OF DEW

Thank you, O Eos,
Lovely Goddess of the Dawn
For the priceless jewels
Left sprinkled upon my lawn.
How the diamonds sparkle
In your early morning glow
As they tremble on the rose
Then nestle in the velvet green below.

DEEPENING LOVE

Like the flowing rivers,
My love for you deepens
With each passing day.

# DAWN OF NIGHT

Against the horizon,
Sail boats two,
The fiery sun's
Half-hidden view.
Fingers of light
Across the sky,
Dawning of night's
Soft lullaby!

## CASTLES

Visions of me and you…
Fairy tales coming true.
Castles in the sky,
Dreamers you and I

# DAWN

Fragile wings of birds that fly~
A soft, tinkling lullaby.
A gentle zephyr from the west…
Dawn – the time I love best!

## CHILDREN'S DELIGHT

Weaving fairy tales in the night,
With goblins and elves and children delight
There are lots of warlocks and witches
And clowns in their funny britches.
Children caught up in total surprise
A look of wonderment in their eyes.

## BEAUTIFUL MEMORIES

Memories, like silver threads,
Echo through my mind.
And with softly whispered words
They're gently entwined.
A wonderful sense of contentment
They always leave behind.

## ASLEEP

Last night while sleeping in my bed,
I woke up and thought I was dead:
And to my amazement, what did I do
But wake up this morning and find it true.

## ALONE

The soft white clouds
In a sky deeply blue
Somehow all remind me
That death has taken you.

The sighing of the wind,
The calmness of the sea
Both seem to gather 'round
To try and comfort me.

Perhaps these lips of mine
will smile again tomorrow…
Today I'm so lost,
Walking alone in my sorrow.

## A TREASURE

You were always there
When I needed a friend.
Your patience was long,
It never had an end.
There was never a charge…
It was always given free.
Thank you for the friendship
You have given to me.

# A PLACE OF LOVE

We walk in love~
You and I…
Suspended forever between
Earth and sky:
So far above all
Those mortal men
That nothing but happiness
Can enter in.

## FOREVER YOU

Sometimes happy,
Sometimes blue,
Always loving,
Forever you!

# THE SETTING SUN

A magical feeling gently settles over the land
While the sun is slowly going down.
And the world is shrouded in a swirling mist
As the sky wears her majestic crown.

# GENTLE BREEZE

Whisper softly little breeze
As you talk to the giant oak trees,
Skip gently across the silver sand
To lovingly caress the flowers that stand.
Playfully scatter the clouds in the sky
Before up to God you finally fly.

# GOSSAMER THINGS

Butterfly wings
Gossamer things.
Sparking dew
Loving you!!!

# HOW SOON

I often look upward
And I sigh
At the eternal beauty
Of the sky;
At the timeless space
Where angels fly
And I wonder just
How soon shall I.

# IS IT TOO LATE?

As the years go swiftly by
I sometimes wonder if I
Have been the person I should
And each new test withstood.
I wonder sometimes if perhaps
I have not often been lapse
In doing everything I could.
Have I done more bad than good?
Have I waited too late to change
Or is it still within my range?

## JUST ME

Please accept me as I am
And not as you want me to be.
Don't make of me a pretense, a sham;
For that's all there is, just me!

# LAUGHING EYES

She looks at the world
Thru those laughing eyes
And the world can only guess
How often she cries.

For no one shall truly
Be able to tell
How much pain and sorrow
She hides so well

Even the Ruler of Destiny
With joy she defies
As she looks at Death
Thru those laughing eyes.

# LIVE AND LET LIVE

It matters not how carefully you drive
To beat the rat race and to stay alive…
To live 'til you're very old and mellow,
You must watch out for the other fellow!

# MORNING

Good morning, Morning,
And how are you today?
My, you're looking lovely
For so early in the day.
You look so fresh and new
Sprinkled with drops of Dew.
Morning, thank you for coming,
Have a nice day, won't you!!

# MY KINGDOM

Lying upon white silvery sands,
My head cradled in my hands;
I watch the silhouettes in the sky,
I hear the seagull's lonely cry.
I see the seashells along the shore--

Left there to decorate Heaven's floor
With conch, coral, and starfish too.
I see exotic flowers and skies of blue.
A sense of peace and tranquility
Surrounds my kingdom by the sea.

# A PERSONAL TIDBIT

A personal tidbit
That I'd like to share
It's hard to act suave
and so debonair
With a gob of bird
poop in your hair!

# My Life

While walking the pathway of life
Oft times I have been told
That in my search for dreams
I have become very bold;
That I have dared to walk
Where Angels fear to tread
And soon coals of wrath
Will be heaped upon my head.
But I must live my life
The only way I know how…
I cannot put on a show:
I live for today, here and now.

# MY LOVE

Brighter than the glare
Of the noonday's sun;
Softer than the night
When the day is done;
Stronger than the force
Of the raging sea!
Love greater than life
Is yours from me!

# NEW LOVE

The most beautiful sight in all the world to me
is two young lovers, hand in hand, laughing with glee.
A rich new life of happiness has opened for you--
You feel as refreshed as an early morning dew.
Each day takes on new meaning, a reason for living;
Not only the taking but a desire also for giving.
It's wonderful to have someone with whom to share
Your every adventure, your smiles, and your care.
It carries with it such a real sense of belonging
That from within your heart now comes thronging
Such an overflowing amount of strength and vitality
That all intricate chores quickly become a finality.
You hurry through each day, which none too soon fades
Into the cherished softness of the dark nightshades.
These are the times you will both remember and smile;
At those secret meetings, you planned with so much guile.
How determined you both were that no one should know
Yet, it wasn't a secret, for your very souls did glow.

# NICE DOGGIE

Take that smile off your face
Baron, My love, My pet;
And, now show me, please
Where you buried the Vet!

# NOT YET, DEATH

Oh, Death, I see you
Lurking there in the
Deepening shadows
With arms outstretched
And hands that beckon to me!

But, Death, I fear that
You have come in vain
For it's much too soon
Of this life
For me to want to be free!

I fear you not, Oh Death,
Nor do I envy
For I still have a lot
Of living to do
And, Death, God is here beside me!

# NOW IS THE TIME

I made you happy
For such a short while;
I gave you laughter
And I made you smile.
But you are still lost
In dreams of yesterday
And it would be cruel
To awaken you today.
So now is the time
For me to move on.
Others will take my place
After I am gone.
Please remember that no matter
How far you fly,
No one shall love you
Better than I.

## Only Yesterday

I have known all of my life
Though I met you only yesterday
You have always been by my side
When times looked dark and grey.
You were ever-present in my dreams;
I know you well, though we met only yesterday.

# OPPORTUNITY'S KNOCK

It really is quite shocking,
To dream of going so very far;
To find it isn't opportunity knocking,
It's something in your car!

# PLEA TO MY FLOWER

Good morning, little flower,
On my window sill.
How beautifully you sit there,
So patiently still.
You're waiting on a drink of water
From someone, I see.
If I give it to you daily,
Won't you please bloom for me?

# RAINY DAY

The clouds are rolling in
Turning blue skies to gray;
Covering up our sunshine,
But it's only for today.

Tomorrow will be sunny;
The gray will all disappear.
Cheer up, my friend, for
Tomorrow is already quite near.

# REQUIEM FOR A DREAM

Weep long for your yesterday
And all those mistakes you made!
Mourn those feet of clay
And truth so long delayed.

Don't be ashamed to cry
For things once held dear;
Let tears blind your eye
And wash away your fear.

Now, yesterday won't be as bad
As once it did seem,
Though it's always mournfully sad;
The death of a Dream.

Now, let those tears fade
Into a memory of yesterday;
Learn from mistakes you made
And dream new dreams today.

## SEASONS OF OUR LOVE

It was early in the springtime
When our love began to grow
It was nothing we had planned
In the beginning, love came slow.
The summertime of our love
Was filled with joy and laughter.
We vowed we'd love each other
Today, tomorrow, in the hereafter.
Our love lingered into the autumn
When old Jack Frost chilled the air.
There were so many things in life
That we could not seem to share.
Then came the icy winds of winter
When only cold and loneliness abide
And like the green leaves of springtime,
Our sweet love, at last, has died.
Like the four seasons of the year,
Our sweet love has come and gone
With only the happiest of our memories
Still lingering on.

## SHARE WITH ME

Come share with me
The moon.
Share all the stars
That shine.
Tomorrow will be here
All too soon,
But tonight is ours;
Yours and mine.

## SILENT TALK

When talking without
Spoken word,
Meanings can never
Be mis-heard.

## SPECIAL

You are that
Special blend:
Rose, orchid
And friend.

## STANDING ALONE

Friends and loved ones we gather round us
From the moment of our birth;
And we want them near us when it is
Our time to leave this Earth.
Yet when the time comes for us to stand
For judgment before God's throne,
It matters not who would walk beside us,
This time we must stand alone.

## SUMMERS PAST

A ghost from
Summers past
Made me smile
Last night;
Beautiful, but it
Couldn't last,
Foolish to think
It might.

## SUNRISE

The fragile fingers of light
Slowly soften the eastern sky.
Softly through the fading night
The birds sing their lullaby.

Glistening in the dreaming dawn,
The sparkling diamonds of dew
Tremble on the velvet lawn
Reflecting morning's rosy hue.

# SUNSET IN PASTEL

The cobweb clouds
Surrounding the sun
With pastel shrouds,
So lightly spun.

The shimmering trail
Across the sea:
The silvery sail
Seen so fleetingly.

The coconut palm
Upon the beach;
Night time magic
Just out of reach.

# THANK YOU, GOD

When each day fades
Into deep night shades;
And the sinking sun slides
Behind the mountainsides;
When the beautiful sunset I see,
I thank my God for Thee.

# THE BLIND

I once knew a man
Who was blind;
He had no eyes with
Which to see.
And yet there were a
Great many things
That he saw much more
Clearly than me.

I saw only what was
Before my eyes
And took no time to
See things apart.
I know now he really
Didn't need eyes--
For he could see things
With his heart.

# THE LIGHT BEYOND

I soared high above the earth
One storm-filled night
And I gazed in rapture at a
Most awesome sight.
I saw the storm clouds roll
And the lightening flash!
I saw the raindrops flow;
I heard the thunder crash!
I felt the violence of the storm
Raging all around!
It filled the earth and sky;
It swept across the ground.
Then as I looked to the right,
God waved his magic wand
And created a miraculous sight;
The moon shining just beyond.

## THE RADIANCE OF YOUTH

Girl, you look at me
With your laughing eyes
And make me wonder
Where your future lies.

What mortal man will steal
Your youthful innocence?
How long will it take
To dim that radiance?

That aura of happiness
Which now surrounds you;
The sense of enchantment
In everything you do!

God, let it last forever
Is my fervent prayer;
Let the sound of laughter
Forever echo there.

## THE SECRET OF LOVING

I know you cannot return
The love I have shown,
For you cannot give
What you do not own;
And I have always found
This to be consistently true:
Before you can truly love others,
You must first love you.

# YOU GAVE ME A SMILE

To me, you are a person very
Precious and so unique.
You have a smile in your voice
Every time that you speak.
You have touched my life in
A multitude of ways--
You have walked along beside me
During the darkest of my days!
And with a simple word, you have
Dried up all of my tears.
You have given me enough happiness
To last a great many years.
You have filled my world with
So much joy and laughter
That it will echo through my mind
For a long time hereafter!
And so, before my time on Earth
Shall come to an end,
I wanted to take time to say to you,
"Thank you, my Friend!

## AS PRETTY

If I'm really as pretty
As you once said,
Then why must I wear
This bag over my head?

## A PERFECT GIFT

I don't need
Your silver and gold
Nor anything else
That's bought and sold.
You may believe this
For it really is true;
Your thoughts and
A smile will do.

# A NEW DAY

The morning after
The night before
I stand expectantly
At my door:
My arms outstretched
A heart that sings:
Anxious to see what
This day brings!

# A FRIEND

When days seem long
And I am feeling low;
When I need a kind word,
You always seem to know.

You are always there
When things go wrong;
You lift up my spirits
And give me a song.

You make me happy
When I'm feeling blue;
And when I need a friend
I always can count on you.

# FROM ME TO YOU

How shall I describe the
Feelings you've aroused within?
For they have no beginning
And yet they have no end!

You reached out and touched
That secret part of me
That so very few people
Shall be allowed to see.

You have introduced to me
A me I did not know.
And it's a beautiful feeling;
One that can only grow.

You taught me to love you
A hundred thousand ways:
During the long, cool nights;
Through the hot, sultry days.

You gave me passion and ecstasy;
Carried me through heights divine.
I love the feel of power in you
When your body is one with mine.

I love the strength in your arms
And the gentleness of your touch.
I love the friendship you gave
Just when I needed it so much.

I love the dark side of you
That you try so hard to hide.
I know that you have a devil
Raging somewhere deep inside.

A devil that you must somehow
Learn to fully, completely control;
For if it is left unleashed,
It will devour your very soul!

And, for anyone who looks with love,
You could never possibly disguise
That look of frustration, hurt and pain--
That total empty sadness in your eyes.

You are such a beautiful person
To be filled with such anger and doubt!
Walk tall wherever your steps may go,
For, in truth, you are man, inside out.

Know that it takes a very strong man
To be as soft and gentle as you!
I know you as companion, lover, friend.
I know you can be crude and selfish too.

Yet I have loved all these things
For it takes all to make the total you.
Whatever you give to life will be returned,
So, before you love others, first love you.

When fate takes us our separate ways,
Totally separate we can never be;
For you can never give to another
That which you have given to me.

It shall remain a part of me forever~~
One I hold sacred, one that I will cherish
Until all the stars shall refuse to shine
And all the breath in me shall perish.

And now though it saddens me
That this should be so~~
As I have learned to love you,
I must learn to let you go!

Our lives will turn full circle;
But now there can be no us, no we~~
Yet go knowing that I would freely,
Lovingly give my life for Thee!!

# MY WILD THANKSGIVING TURKEY

My turkey shot out of the oven
And rocketed through the air;
It knocked every plate off the table
And partly demolished a chair!
It then ricocheted into a corner and
Burst with a deafening BOOM!
It splattered all over the kitchen,
Completely covering the room.
It stuck to the walls and the windows
And totally coated the floor--
There was turkey attached to the ceiling
Where there's never been turkey before!
It blanketed every appliance,
It coated every saucer and bowl,
There was no way I could stop it--
That turkey was OUT OF CONTROL!
I prayed as I scraped and cleaned
And I vowed as the floor I mopped--
That never again will I stuff a turkey
With popcorn that hadn't been popped!

# THE END

# About Mary E. Fisher

I have been fascinated by words for as long as I can remember. So much so that a few years ago I decided that I wanted to learn every word in the dictionary. I wanted to learn spelling, enunciation, and correct usage.

Unfortunately, other demands and obligations required more of my time so that pursuit was postponed before I progressed very far.

In high school, I was asked to tutor some of my classmates as well as students in higher grades, wherever they had a weakness, during my study periods.

Several years ago I was honored to be chosen one of the nominees as Poet Laureate of the State of Florida, however, I was not selected.

I have written and directed multiple short plays which were very well received... in addition, I wrote the lyrics of several songs, two of which were recorded and aired on many radio stations.

www.ingramcontent.com/pod-product-compliance
Lightning Source LLC
LaVergne TN
LVHW021544080426
835509LV00019B/2831